Richard Claverhouse, Sir, Jebb

Humanism in education

Richard Claverhouse, Sir, Jebb

Humanism in education

ISBN/EAN: 9783743306585

Manufactured in Europe, USA, Canada, Australia, Japa

Cover: Foto ©ninafisch / pixelio.de

Manufactured and distributed by brebook publishing software
(www.brebook.com)

Richard Claverhouse, Sir, Jebb

Humanism in education

.

HUMANISM IN EDUCATION.

PETRARCH was born in 1304, when Dante was thirty-nine years old, and died in 1374. That great movement in which he was a pioneer, and which we call the Renaissance, had its central inspiration in the belief that the classical literatures, which were being gradually recovered, were the supreme products of the human mind; that they were the best means of self-culture; that there alone one could see the human reason moving freely, the moral nature clearly expressed, in a word, the dignity of man, as a rational being, fully displayed. All this is implied in humanism, when we speak of humanism as the direction in which the Renaissance chiefly tended. It is larger than the Roman idea of *humanitas*; the scope of which is well illustrated by Cicero when he says in one of his letters that Roman officials ought to treat Greeks with 'humanitas' (gentleness), since it is from Greece that Italy first received 'humanitas,'—i.e., as the context explains, the refining influences of literature and art.

It is difficult adequately to realize now the whole meaning of humanism for the early Renaissance, because we cannot quite place ourselves within the mental horizon of the middle ages. We know, in a general way, what was the intellectual background of the Renaissance; the dominance of the scholastic philosophy in the thirteenth century; the prominent position held by the studies of Law and Medicine; the comparative poverty and inefficiency of the higher literary studies for, though portions of the best Latin classics continued to be read throughout the middle ages they were read, as a rule, in a spirit remote from the classical, or even contrary to it; and the West had lost Greek altogether. But such facts do not help us far towards entering into the heart of the early Renaissance. Perhaps there are two men who more than any others, assist the effort to do so; Dante, standing in the borderland between the darker ages and the revival, when he shows us a keen intellect and a sublime imagination moving within the limits, and obedient to the forms, of medieval thought; and, at the further verge of the Renaissance, Erasmus, the lifelong antagonist of the schoolmen, who makes so vivid to us the contrast between the intellectual atmosphere of scholasticism and that which the humane letters had created.

Petrarch.   Petrarch opens an era, because he was the first man in medieval Europe, not perhaps who possessed but who was able effectively and impressively to manifest, a strong native affinity with the genius of the classical Latin writers; the first who succeeded in making large numbers of people feel that he had studied those writers with intelligent enthusiasm, and that they were to him living persons. Resembling Goethe in his steadfast pursuit of a complete self-culture, Petrarch proclaimed that the classics supply the best, the unique, instrument for that purpose. He enjoyed in Italy an immense popularity and renown ; his Latin epic poem, ' Africa,' though often tame, won scarcely less applause than his Italian lyrics ; and his Latin prose-writings were widely read. .He was also the first man of, great eminence who showed zeal in collecting books, manuscripts, and coins. He did not know Greek ; yet, with a sure instinct, he apprehended its significance, and was eager that the knowledge of it should be restored. The age must have been ready for the movement ; but it was the powerful and famous personality of Petrarch which gave the initial impulse. His devoted disciple, who died only one year later (in 1375), the gentle and diligent Boccaccio, earliest of Italian Hellenists, propagated and diffused Petrarch's influence ; and so, before the close of the fourteenth century, the full tide of the humanistic revival had set in.

Petrarch's ideal of humanism, as a discipline which aims at drawing out all the mental and moral faculties of man, pervades the whole course of the Italian Renaissance. Often, indeed, that ideal was obscured by affectations or puerilities ; not seldom it was belied by evil living ; but nevertheless it was a real force, which comes out more or less in all the greater and nobler of the humanists. The enthusiasm

Persistence of his ideal.

and the versatile energy which animated the Italian
Renaissance for two centuries sprang from a deep
and earnest conviction that the 'recovered literatures
were not only models of style, but treasure-houses
of wisdom, guides of life, witnesses to a civilisation
higher than any which could then be found upon the
earth. Even in the early years of the sixteenth
century, when the best energies of the movement
had in Italy been spent, and when Italian humanism
was being narrowed down from the ample scholarship of Politian to the Ciceronian purism of Bembo,
this fundamental belief remained unaltered.

One illustration may be cited. In the year 1508,
a manuscript containing the first six (or, as then
constituted, the first five) books of the Annals of
Tacitus, said to have been found in the Westphalian
monastery of Corbey, was brought to Rome, and
was acquired by Giovanni de' Medici, who, five
years later, became Leo X. It is the only manuscript of those books which exists, and is now in the
Laurentian Library at Florence. One of Leo's
earliest acts, after he became Pope, was to entrust
the printing of this codex to a scholar of note,
Filippo Beroaldo the younger, whose edition was
published at Rome in 1515. As a reward to the
editor, Leo conferred upon him a privilege for the
sale and reprinting of the work. In the brief which
grants this privilege, and which is prefixed to the
edition, Leo expresses his estimate of humanistic
studies. 'We have been accustomed,' he says, 'even
from our early years, to think that nothing more

Leo X. on humanism.

excellent or more useful has been given by the Creator to mankind, if we except only the knowledge and true worship of Himself, than these studies, which not only lead to the ornament and guidance of human life, but are applicable and useful to every particular situation; in adversity consolatory, in prosperity pleasing and honourable; insomuch, that without them we should be deprived of all the grace of life and all the polish of social intercourse.' He goes on to say that 'the security and extension of these studies' seem to depend chiefly on two things, —'the number of men of learning, and the ample supply of excellent authors.' As to the first, it has always been his earnest desire to encourage men of letters; and as to the acquisition of books, he rejoices when an opportunity is afforded him of thus 'promoting the advantage of mankind.' It would be a mistake to discount such language as conventional. Whatever else in the literary fashions of that time may have been hollow, this feeling, at least, as to the value of the classics, was thoroughly real.

I have insisted on this larger scope of the Renaissance humanism, because we are naturally apt to think of it as having been primarily a cult of style and form, an effort to imitate and reproduce the excellence of the ancient models. And of course this was one of its chief aims,—nay, perhaps, the most characteristic of the special activities which the revival called forth. But we should be in danger of taking this *imitatio veterum* for something less significant than it really was, if we did not

Stylistic side of humanism.

remember the point of view from which the Italian
humanists approached it. They regarded the
ancient Romans as their forefathers, and Latin as
their ancestral speech. During the dark ages, the
old civilisation had been effaced, the language had
been barbarized : if they could not restore the
civilisation, they wished at least to regain the
language which attested it. Medieval Italy had
many dialects ; the literary Tuscan had only a
limited currency, while Latin was the universal
language. Not long after Dante's death in 1321,
the 'Divine Comedy' was translated into Latin.
The eminent humanist Francesco Filelfo, who died
in 1481 at the age of eighty-three, could still say,
'Tuscan is hardly known to all Italians, while Latin
is spread far and wide throughout the whole world.'
Thus, in the effort to purify and elevate Latin style,
patriotic sentiment and practical convenience con-
spired with the newborn zeal of scholarship.

During the interval between the middle of the
fourteenth century and the earlier part of the sixteenth, a long series of humanists cultivated Latin
prose-writing in every branch,—oratory, philosophical
discourse, diplomatic or official correspondence,
familiar letter-writing. The stress laid on the
niceties of the art is shown by the reputation which
Lorenzo Valla, best known as the translator of
Thucydides, owed to his work called *Elegantiae*,
published in 1432—1436. In the generation after
his, Politian wrote Latin like a living language.
Then the dictatorship passed to Bembo, prince of

Latin prose-
writing.

those Ciceronians whom Erasmus derides. It is
easy to make light of such work, but it is better and
more important to remember what it was that the
humanists achieved in this way. One of our poets
has described Dante's immortal poem as ' The first
words Italy had said'; and if Dante was the first
who found a voice for Italian literature, medieval
Latin had altogether failed to preserve the clearness
or beauty of classical expression. When Petrarch's
contemporaries compared themselves with their
Roman predecessors, they felt that they were in-
articulate. To write their ancestral tongue with
clearness, in the first place, and then with some
measure of grace or beauty,—this became to them
an object of ardent desire. Gradually, and by
painful efforts, they attained it. And thereby they
bequeathed to Europe a tradition which the middle
ages had lost,—namely, that prose, in whatever
language it may be written, should aim at those
qualities which the best classical models exhibit.
This is the permanently valuable result of the
humanistic Latin prose-writing.

As to their copious Latin verse, if there is Latin verse.
not much of it which deserves to live, unquestion-
ably it served to cultivate in many men a genuine
poetical gift; it was the vehicle of much graceful
fancy and much fine perception ; and it conduced
to a closer study of the best Latin poets. In force
and spontaneity, though not in delicacy or finish,
Politian is the most remarkable of the Renaissance versifiers. He was only forty when he died

in 1494, and a still youthful fire breathes in his impetuous hexameters. When he was lecturing at Florence, he sometimes began by reciting a Latin poem of his own, as an introduction to the classical author. Some of these poems, in hexameter verse, remain. One of them rapidly surveys the history of poetry from Homer to Boccaccio; another is a prelude to the 'Iliad' and 'Odyssey'; a third, to the bucolic poets, especially Hesiod and Virgil. In these, as in much other Latin verse of the Renaissance, despite some blemishes which modern scholarship would have avoided, one can see how thoroughly the writer was imbued with the style of diction of his models. A fine ear is a frequent Italian gift, and some of these Renaissance versifiers have been singularly successful in catching the rhythms of the best Latin poets, especially those of Virgil and of Ovid.

The Italian humanists' desire of fame : Verse and rhetoric were, indeed, modes of self-expression irresistibly attractive to men whose ambition was fired by the example of their Italian ancestors, and who felt that motive so characteristic of the Renaissance,—the passionate desire of the individual to make his own powers stand out, clear-cut and brilliant, before the world,—the longing for fame in his life-time, and for the praise of posterity. Italy had no political unity, no common its national aspect. aims in respect to national life. Humanism proposed what to many men, and coteries, and cities took, in a way, the place of that,—the dream that the glories

another golden age of letters and art. That vision
dawned upon Petrarch in a peaceful time, when, in
his poem 'Africa,' he predicted that the new love
for the Muses would rival the old ; and it continued
to cheer students amidst all the foreign invasions
and intestine troubles which crowded upon Italy
two centuries later. After the sack of Rome in
1527, and when the condition of Italy on every side
was deplorable, an accomplished scholar, Marcan-
tonio Flaminio, sent to his patron, Alessandro
Farnese, a collection of Latin poems by natives of
Lombardy, which was then the region in which
letters chiefly flourished. In some verses which
accompanied this gift, he cries : 'Happy, too happy,
are our days, which have given birth to a Catullus,
a Tibullus, a Horace, and a Virgil of their own !'

The Italian humanists' cult of style was thus
connected with a larger aim, that of regaining a lost
culture, regarded as ancestral ; and it did a work of
lasting value for European literature. But we owe
to them much more than that. We owe to them,
for instance, that conception, ever present to the
stronger men in their ranks, of classical antiquity as
a whole. The outlook of the greater humanists was
a wide one. Filelfo, already mentioned, was a
typical scholar of the fifteenth century: when he
was professor at Florence, about 1428, he lectured
in the morning on Cicero, then on Livy, or Homer :
in the afternoon, on Terence, followed by Thucydides. Meanwhile, among other private labours,
he translated into Latin Aristotle's 'Rhetoric,'

Their wide
range.

some speeches of Lysias, extracts from Xenophon, and some of Plutarch's 'Lives.' Politian edited Catullus in his youth, and the Pandects of Justinian in his riper age: published notes on Ovid and Statius, on Suetonius, the younger Pliny, Quintilian and other Latin authors; made Latin translations from Hippocrates, Plato, Herodian, and Galen. Erasmus became to northern Europe the prophet of this comprehensive humanism in its educational and also in its more popular aspects. Such largeness of range and view, albeit obtained at some sacrifice of other qualities, is, in its own way, an intellectual gain.

To another service of the humanists, one which is more apt to be forgotten, it must suffice to allude in passing,—I mean what they did for erudition, as distinguished from literary scholarship. Their commentaries, their works on antiquities of every kind, have mostly been absorbed or superseded; but in these provinces also the later learning must acknowledge a vast debt. Flavio Biondo, who died in 1463, deserves to be remembered as one of the chief founders of Roman archæology, in virtue of his threefold work, 'Roma Instaurata,' 'Roma Triumphans,' and 'Italia Illustrata.' The study of Latin epigraphy, again, received a notable benefit from Jacopo Mazochi and his collaborator Albertini, who, building partly on earlier collections, published in 1521 their 'Inscriptions of Rome.' It was under the direct influence of humanism that the first Roman Museums of anti-

Their erudite work. (margin note)

quities and art were formed,—those of the Capitol and of the Vatican.

But Italian humanism has a claim on our grati-tude even larger and higher than its work for scholarship and for erudition, great and varied as that work was. Europe owes to humanism the creation of a new atmosphere, the diffusion of a new spirit, the initiation of forces hostile to obscur-antism, pedantry and superstition, forces making for intellectual light, for the advance of knowledge in every field, and not merely for freedom, but for something without which freedom itself may be a burden or a curse, the power to comprehend its right limits and to employ it for worthy ends. Take a particular instance. In the fourteenth and fifteenth centuries, the so-called science of Astrology held an exceedingly strong position. Universities endowed it with Chairs; kings and princes consulted the stars in crises of State; a general in the field was not seldom accompanied by his astrologer; cities and citizens had recourse to horoscopes in countless affairs of municipal or private life. But from Petrarch onwards the humanists made open war on this flourishing im-posture. Or take another illustration of a some-what different kind. That vigorous and versatile humanist, Poggio, was at the Council of Constance in 1416, and heard Jerome of Prague recant his recantation. Poggio was then, and had been for many years, a lay secretary in the Papal Chancery. But he does not think of Jerome as of a heretic at bay. With a detachment which would have been scarcely possible for a medieval spectator of similar antecedents, Poggio is able to contemplate Jerome simply as a man who is evincing heroic fortitude —and thus describes him in a letter to Lionardo Bruni :—' There he stood, undismayed, unfaltering, not merely indifferent to death, but ready to welcome it,—another Cato.'

Humanistic education.

It was impossible that men penetrated by this new spirit, and for whom the new learning was the revelation of a new life, should not soon apply their ideas to the training of the young. Within fifty years after the death of Petrarch, we find a type of education developed which, in contrast with the medieval, may be called the humanistic. It is, in its essentials, a type which satisfied the western world for four hundred years; the generation has not yet passed away which first saw its claims seriously challenged; and its origins must always have for us more than an ordinary measure of historical interest. Among the great teachers of the earlier Renaissance, there is one who has a pre-eminent right to be regarded as the founder of this education, and of him a few words must be said here; I refer to Vittorino da Feltre.

Vittorino da Feltre.

Born in 1378 at Feltre, a small town in Venetia, he went at eighteen to the University of Padua, then second in Italy only to Bologna, and sharing with Pavia the distinction, still rare at that time in Universities, of being comparatively favourable to humanism. He there studied Latin under two

eminent masters in succession, Giovanni da Ra-
venna, and Gasparino Barzizza,—the latter a great
Ciceronian scholar, but exempt from the narrow
purism of a later time. Another Paduan teacher
whose influence Vittorino must have felt was
Vergerius, already celebrated for his essay on
the formation of character ('De Ingenuis Mori-
bus'),—the earliest and most lucid statement of
the principles on which humanistic training rested ;
an essay which, amidst the throng of Renaissance
treatises on education, remained a classic for two
centuries, going through some forty editions before
the year 1600. Vittorino, after holding a chair
of Rhetoric at Padua, and then teaching privately
at Venice, was invited by Gian Francesco Gonzaga,
Marquis of Mantua, to undertake the tuition of
his children. A villa was assigned to him at
Mantua, where he was to reside with his pupils.
He settled there in 1425, and remained till his
death in 1446. The villa had been of the most
luxurious kind, and was known as the 'House of
Pleasure' ('La Gioiosa') ; Vittorino, by a slight but
meaning change, named it the 'Pleasant House'
('La Giocosa') ; banished the luxury which had
environed the young Gonzagas ; and turned the
place into a seat of plain living and regular study.
But he was a thorough believer in bright sur-
roundings as conducive to mental and moral health.
The house was cheerful and beautiful ; it stood in
large grounds, fringed by a river ; there was ample
space and provision for every kind of outdoor

exercise or sport. Youths were sent from several
of the Italian Courts to be educated with the
Mantuan princes. But Vittorino was resolved that
the school should be open to any boy who was
fitted to profit by it, and maintained at his own
cost a large number of poor scholars, for whom
lodgings were found near the villa. The rules of
life and study were the same for all.

Vittorino's
aim.

Vittorino's aim in education was to develope and
train the whole nature of his pupil, intellectual, moral
and physical; and to do this, not with a view to any
special calling, but so as to form good citizens, useful
members of society, men capable of bearing their
part with credit in public and private life. This
being his general aim, let us see how his methods
differed from those which had prevailed in the
middle ages, and in what sense they may be described as humanistic. In the pre-Renaissance
schools for boys, the dominant influence was ecclesiastical. In teaching grammar and rhetoric, portions
of the Latin classics were used; but the method
of teaching them was encumbered with fantastic
pedantry,—such, for instance, as the doctrine that a
passage may have four meanings, literal, metaphori-
cal, allegorical, and mystical,—which went far to
annul their value and meaning as literature. For
that value and that meaning an enthusiastic appreciation came in with the humanistic revival; to the
humanist, the great writers of antiquity were living
men, into whose mind and soul he was striving to
penetrate by sympathetic study. That was the

spirit in which Vittorino **took the Latin** classics, His use of
and made them **the basis of** intellectual training. the classics;
Poetry, oratory, history, **the ethics of** Roman Stoic-
ism, were studied in the best Latin writers. And,
if not at first, yet before **he had** been many years
at Mantua, Vittorino introduced some Greek classics
also. His **own** knowledge of that language **was**
chiefly due to his contemporary, **the other** great
schoolmaster of **the** time, **Guarino of** Verona.
Guarino had studied **Greek at Constantinople,** and
shares with Vittorino **the honour of having** established Greek as **a regular part of liberal** education
in schools. Vittorino's scholars were constantly
practised in Greek **and** Latin composition, **as well**
as in recitation and reading aloud.

But, while classical literature was thus the basis and of other
of Vittorino's system, **it** was by no means his only subjects.
subject. Aided by resident tutors, he taught mathematics, including geometry (a subject which the
humanists preferred **to** the schoolmen's **logic)** and
arithmetic, with rudiments **of astronomy; also, it**
seems, some elements **of what** then **passed for**
Natural Philosophy **and Natural** History. Music
and singing also found a place, though under conditions which Plato **and Aristotle** would **have**
approved ; the standard **of attainment** aimed at was
to be that of the amateur, **not of the** professional ;
and **the** music **was** to be chosen with regard
to its moral effect. Nor was social education
neglected : Vittorino inculcated a noble tone of
manners, and **desired** that **his pupils** should have

such accomplishments as would enable them to grace social life.

Physical training. As to physical training, he provided instructors in military exercises, in riding, and in swimming, while he encouraged every form of healthy outdoor activity. In all this he was the typical humanist. The ecclesiastical schoolmaster of the middle ages was not concerned to encourage physical training; the opinion was rather that the body was something to be despised and mortified. The medieval provision for such training was not in schools but in the households of princes or nobles, where riding, tilting, the chase, and other martial or courtly exercises were practised. On the physical and the social sides of his scheme Vittorino was in some sort continuing this old court training; many of his pupils, indeed, were nobles destined to the profession **Dominant** of arms. But the idea which dominated his whole **idea of** system was the classical, originally Greek, idea of **humanistic** **education:** an education in which mind and body should be harmoniously developed. No antique idea appealed with greater force to the humanists, since none presented a stronger contrast to medieval theory and practice. When we give the name of humanistic to the type of education established by Vittorino and his contemporaries, it is not simply or chiefly because the intellectual part of it was based on Greek and Latin, but, in a more important sense, because the education was at once intellectual, moral, and physical.

With reference to moral teaching, it should be

said that Vittorino, unlike many of the humanists, was an orthodox, even a devout, Churchman, an earnestly religious man, whose precepts were enforced by his practice. Like almost all the great humanist teachers, he was a layman, engaged in creating a type of education which might be contrasted with the ecclesiastical type that had preceded it : but there was no tinge of paganism in his view of religion or of ethics : he was one of those men who, like Pico della Mirandola, recognised the unity of knowledge,—separated the gold of the new treasure-trove from the dross,—and neither felt nor sought any conflict between the classical and the Christian ideal.

It is interesting for Englishmen to remember that Winchester College was built in Vittorino's boyhood, and that the Mantuan public school was at its zenith when Henry VI. founded Eton. Both those illustrious foundations, since so distinguished as seats of humanistic training, arose before humanism had come to England, and were originally of the ecclesiastical type. Towards the end of the fifteenth century, a few Oxford scholars, who had visited Italy,—William Selling, Grocyn, William Latimer, Thomas Linacre,—brought the taste for humane letters to England, where it was presently quickened by the visits of Erasmus. St Paul's School, founded by the friend of Erasmus, Dean Colet, is the oldest in England which was humanistic from its origin. Its first High Master, William Lily, of Magdalen College, appointed by the

Early humanism in English schools.

founder in 1512, is best remembered as a Latin grammarian, but had also studied Greek at Rhodes and afterwards at Rome. It might almost be said that the relation in which St Paul's School stood to the influence of the earliest Oxford humanists resembled that in which Vittorino's school at Mantua stood to the early humanism of Florence.

The statutes of St Paul's, dated 1518, prescribe that the High Master shall be 'learned in good and clean Latin, and also in Greek, if such may be gotten.' The proviso is significant. Several great public schools were founded, or re-founded, in or near London, during the century which followed; —Christ's Hospital in 1533, Westminster in 1560, Merchant Taylors' in 1561, Charterhouse in 1611; and in all of these, as in many smaller grammar-schools founded at the same period, the basis was humanistic. But it was probably not much before 1560 that Greek was thoroughly established among English school studies. The statutes of Harrow School, dated 1590, contain directions for the teaching of some Greek orators and historians, and of Hesiod. This seems to be one of the earliest English examples of detailed regulations, as distinguished from merely general prescription, concerning the school study of Greek.

Classical learning since the Renaissance. The resources of humanism as an instrument of education have been expanded and enriched by the manifold development of the higher classical learning in the centuries since the Renaissance. After the age of Petrarch, of Politian, of Erasmus, came

Joseph Scaliger, akin, on the literary side of his work, to the Italian scholars, but more characteristically occupied in the endeavour to frame a critical chronology of the ancient world ; Casaubon, the first who popularized a connected knowledge of ancient life and manners ; Bentley, active primarily in the emendation of texts, but also in the higher criticism of classical history and literature ; then a long series of eminent names, too long to enumerate, which extends from the days of Porson and Elmsley, of Hermann and Lachmann, to those of Mommsen. Within the last fifty years, many special branches of classical study have either sprung into existence, or become more methodical ; comparative philology ; epigraphy ; palæography ; archæology in all its departments. In quite recent times, the exploration of ancient sites, stimulated by, and in turn stimulating, archæological research, has yielded results of fascinating interest. All these developments have lent new life and freshness to classical studies generally : they have given a more vivid reality to antiquity. The ideal of humanism has thus been reinforced in a manner which brings back to us something of the spirit which animated the Renaissance when it was largest and most vigorous. For the enthusiasm of the Renaissance was nourished by the monuments of classical art scarcely less than by the masterpieces of literature. Each statue that was disinterred from Italian soil, every stone or coin or gem that could help to illustrate the past, became a source of delight to men whose strenuous aim was to apprehend classical antiquity as a whole.

Humanism and specialization.

But the very progress made in recent times has brought us to a point at which the larger educational benefits of humanism become more difficult to harmonise with the new standards of special knowledge. A full comprehension of the Greek and Latin literatures demands at least *some* study of ancient thought, ancient history, archæology, art. But each of the latter subjects is now, in itself, an organized and complex discipline; to become an expert in any one of them is a work of years. Hence much can be said in favour of a plan by which the University student, who is to devote a course of three or four years to the humane letters, confines himself, during the earlier stage of it, to the languages and literatures; then turns away from these, viewed in their wider range, and concentrates himself, for the rest of his time, on one or two important aspects of classical antiquity, such as philosophy and history, to the exclusion of the rest.

The younger student, in the highest form of a school where the classics are taught, has not yet reached the moment at which the need of specializing begins to be felt. We will suppose that he has an aptitude and taste for literary studies; and the number of such boys is always very considerable—immensely larger, for instance, than the number of those who are fitted to excel in Greek or Latin composition. When he first attains to some appreciation of the best classical poetry and prose, he

goes through a little Renaissance of his own ; he
feels the stimulus of discovery ; he perceives, in
some measure, a beauty of form unlike anything
that he has found elsewhere ; there is much in the
thoughts of those great writers, much of their charm,
much of their music, that fixes itself in his memory,
and becomes part of his consciousness. However dimly and imperfectly, there lives before him
a world very distinct from that in which he moves,
and yet, as he can already feel, by no means
wholly alien from it ; though perhaps he does not
yet understand with any clearness the nature of the
links which bind that past to the present. This,
as many masters and pupils could testify, is an
experience not confined to the school-boy of ex-
ceptional temperament or gifts ; it is one common
to a fairly large proportion of boys who have no
more than a good average capacity for literary
studies in general. And it is an experience which
is not forgotten afterwards. Whatever the man's
work may be in after years, if ever he looks back
and tries to date epochs in his mental history, he
will recur to that early time as a season which made
the buds unfold and the leaves grow, which gave
him new elements of intellectual life and interest.
Ver illud erat.

But the conditions under which that early
experience was gained are modified when the
student passes to the University. It may be
that he works under a system which permits him
to devote the whole of his academic course to

the classical languages and literatures; if so, the humanistic training begun at school is carried to a certain maturity; but it remains exclusively literary. If, on the other hand, he turns, at a certain point, from the general study of the languages and literatures to one or two special subjects, such as ancient philosophy and history, then he is expected to aim at the standards set by modern specialists in those subjects. That through these subjects he can receive an admirable intellectual training, is not disputed. But his range of view is necessarily contracted. The particular educational merits which belong to humanistic studies of a larger scope are different in kind from those which can be claimed for any special department of such studies when isolated from the rest. It may be added that, when specialization has been carried far in any study of literature or art, that study tends

· to become technical; and then a danger arises lest the pursuit of exact method should obscure the nature of the material with which the study has to deal, namely, productions of human thought and imagination; there is a danger lest analogies drawn from studies conversant with different material should be pushed too far, and what is called the scientific spirit should cease to be duly tempered by æsthetic and literary judgment.

We remember what Gibbon so characteristically said about his early mathematical studies: 'As soon as I understood the principles, I relinquished for ever the pursuit of the mathematics; nor can I lament that I desisted before my mind was hardened by the habit of rigid demonstration, so destructive of the finer feelings of moral evidence.' Might not something analogous be said about some of those ultra-technical aspects which some special departments of classical study occasionally present, when we consider these in relation to the nature and the ends of humane literature? No one will suspect me of underrating the immense services which have been rendered to classical study, in every department, by deeper and more thorough work, by rational and exact methods of research. I only say that the tendency to make those methods too technical is one of the besetting temptations of the higher and more esoteric classical study,—a fashion in which it sometimes appears even to exult, as though it were a warning to the profane to stay outside ; and I say that such a tendency is adverse to the appropriate and sympathetic treatment of any subject-matter derived from literature or art. Aristotle observes in the 'Rhetoric' that a speaker unconsciously but inevitably passes out of the province of that art if he begins to reason in the technical terms of a particular science ; and one feels that the modern specialist, in certain branches of classical study, may come perilously near to passing out of the province of humanism.

At any rate, I suppose it would be generally agreed that one of the chief problems which we have to face in classical studies at the present day is this :—How are the characteristic and essential

benefits of humanism to be reconciled with the
learned and intellectual demand for specialization ?
It would not be my desire, even if the occasion
permitted, to attempt a detailed criticism of any
particular answer to that question which has taken
shape and is now operative in this country.   But
one is tempted to ask whether the advance of
knowledge and the subdivision of the field have
really made it impossible to obtain, in the education
of University students, something nearer to that
more comprehensive survey of classical antiquity at
which the earlier humanists aimed.   It may be a
dream, but it is an interesting subject of speculation.
Evidently we have to reckon, at the outset, with
a prepossession which the growth of high specializing has strengthened; namely, that the only intel-
lectually valuable knowledge of a subject is such
as is possessed by the specialist, the expert, in
that subject; and that the acquisition of knowledge which is not, in that sense, thorough can be
of little or no worth, either as a discipline or as a
result.

Now, the most general recommendation of all
classical study is the supreme and varied excellence of the classical literatures ; these illustrate,
and are illustrated by, all the activities of classical
thought and life.   A conceivable ideal of humanistic
study under modern conditions—whether it be prac-
ticable or not, I do not venture to pronounce, though
I am not convinced that it is impracticable—would
be one which took those literatures as the basis

throughout, but also exacted some measure of acquaintance with each of the more important among the other subjects of classical study. Take, for example, the subject of classical art, which means primarily and chiefly Greek art. Even a limited knowledge of that subject is obviously of the greatest value to a student of classical literature ; not merely, of course, as a key to allusions, but often in a far deeper sense, as throwing light on the spirit which animates both monuments and books. I repeat, even a limited knowledge of classical art has that use,—a knowledge which stops far short of the equipment requisite for a specialist in the subject. But, because it is limited, must it therefore be superficial or unsound ? It is difficult to see why it must be so. The teacher to whom students of the classical literatures would have recourse in this matter would be the specialist in classical art. Would he not be competent to decide what parts of his own subject are the most essential for such students to know ? And would he not be competent to secure that, in those selected parts, and within the limits which he himself had traced, the knowledge should not be unsound or superficial ? Like considerations apply to other special departments.

I must be content to have asked this question, and leave the judgment upon it to others. I turn now to the brief consideration of a larger question. What is the general position of the humane letters in this country at the present day, and what are their prospects of retaining that position ? The most salient feature in the intellectual development of this century has been the progress of science. And this century is the first since the revival of learning in which a serious challenge has been thrown down to the defenders of the humanistic tradition. But I think it will be found that the

position of humanism in this country at the close of the century is much stronger than it was at the beginning.

In the earlier part of the century, the classics still held a virtual monopoly, so far as literary studies were concerned, in the public schools and Universities.   And they had no cause to be ashamed of their record.   The culture which they supplied, while limited in the sphere of its operation, had long been an efficient and vital influence, not only in forming men of letters and learning, but in training men who afterwards gained distinction in public life and in various active careers.   There can be no better proof that such a discipline has penetrated the mind, and has been assimilated, than if, in the crises of life, a man recurs to the great thoughts and images of the literature in which he has been trained, and finds there what braces and fortifies him, a comfort, an inspiration, an utterance for his deeper feelings. Robert Wood, in his 'Essay on the Original Genius of Homer' (1769), relates a story which will illustrate what I mean.   In 1762, at the end of the Seven Years' War, Wood, being then an Under-Secretary of State, took the preliminary articles of the Treaty of Paris to the

President of the Council, Lord Granville; who was then ill, and had, indeed, but a few days to live. Seeing what his condition was, Wood proposed to withdraw; but the statesman replied that it could not prolong his life to neglect his duty, and then quoted in Greek from the 'Iliad,' the words of Sarpedon to Glaucus:—'Ah, friend, if, once escaped from this battle, we were for ever to be ageless and immortal, I would not myself fight in the foremost ranks, nor would I send thee into the war that giveth men renown; but now,—since ten thousand fates of death beset us every way, and these no mortal may escape or avoid,—*now let us go forward.*' He repeated the last word, ἴομεν, 'let us go forward,' several times, says Wood, 'with a calm and determinate resignation'; and then, after a pause, asked to hear the Treaty read. That is what I meant by a man recurring, in a crisis of life, to the great thoughts of the literature on which he has been nourished. Or, to give one other example: what a forcible testimony to the hold which this discipline could retain on a congenial spirit is afforded by such a man as the Marquis Wellesley, when, at the close of his career, he addresses his old school in those exquisite Latin elegiacs which can be read in the Chapel of Eton College, where he lies buried,—the lines beginning,

> Fortunae rerumque vagis exercitus undis,
> In gremium redeo serus, Etona, tuum.

It was Eton, he says, which had taught him to aim

high, and to approach the bright fountains of the
ancient wisdom,—*et purum antiquae lucis adire
iubar*; to her he owes whatever he has achieved,
and from her he asks a final resting-place.

Yes, to such men the humanities had been a
true culture ; but the social sphere within which
they gave that culture had been, as I have said,
— limited. And in the earlier years of this century
there arose in English letters no popular force
tending to spread a recognition of the humanistic
ideal. In our imaginative literature the most potent
forces, those which exerted the widest influence,
were then on the side of the romanticists. The
genius of Walter Scott was of course essentially
romantic ; so, too, was that of Byron, his interest in
Greece notwithstanding. Only a very limited
audience was in those days commanded by the
writers whose genius had a native kinship with the
classical, such as Keats and Landor. But a little
later came Tennyson, whose influence throughout
the English-speaking world has made strongly for
an appreciation of the classical spirit, not only
directly, through his poems on classical themes, but
also generally, by his qualities of form and style.
— And the influence of Matthew Arnold, both as a
poet and as a critic, if less widely popular than
Tennyson's, has had a not less penetrating and
subtle power in making the Greek spirit, and the
distinctive qualities of the best Greek achieve-
ment, understood and felt by cultivated readers.
Then, in the domain of history, Grote's great work,

the work of a man of affairs, has done much, more perhaps than any other one book of the century, to invest his subject with a vivid, an almost modern interest for a world wider than the academic, and has done so all the more effectively just because his own antecedents were not academic. Again, there has been a considerable literature, the growth chiefly of the last forty years, which has sought to popularize the classical literatures in a scholarly sense, and to illustrate them from the modern,—such books as those of the late Mr Symonds and the late Professor Sellar. To these must be added translations of the higher order, such as that by which Professor Jowett has made Plato an English classic.

Further, there has been a most remarkable stimulation of interest in classical topography, archæology, and art. New facilities of travel have enabled thousands to become acquainted with the scenes of Greek and Roman life. The study of classical antiquity has been in many respects revolutionized by a series of striking discoveries in Greece, Asia Minor, and Egypt. The opportunities of exploration for English students have been improved by the establishment in 1883 of a school at Athens, which may probably be followed, ere long, by the opening of a similar school at Rome. The wealth of the British Museum in classical antiquities has received frequent accessions; it was never before so attractive or so well organized as a place of classical study. The Universities have meanwhile done much to improve their

3

resources for the study of classical archæology and art.

In all these ways, the humanistic studies have, during this century, become wider and more real. They have gradually been drawn out of a scholastic isolation, and have been brought more and more into the general current of intellectual and literary interests. So far from losing strength or efficacy by ceasing to hold that more exclusive position which they occupied two or three generations ago, they have acquired a fresh vigour, a larger sphere of genuine activity, and a place in the higher education which is more secure, because the acceptance on which it rests is more intelligent.

The critical moment a generation ago. There was, indeed, a moment in this century when the attack upon the humanities was somewhat formidable. It was rather more than thirty years ago, towards the end of the period during which the classics had enjoyed a virtual monopoly in literary education. The educational claims of science had been fully developed, and were being powerfully urged by champions of whom Professor Huxley was the most brilliant ; but these claims had not yet been effectively recognised by adequate provision for the teaching of science in schools and Universities. Several able men, who had been trained in classical studies and had been successful in them, were discontented with the classical system, were conscious of personal needs which it had not satisfied, and felt a sort of resentment against it. In education, as in other matters, some of these men were advanced and eager reformers, who, by their general habit of mind, apart from their particular complaints against the classics, were unlikely to feel any prejudice in favour of tradition,—were apt to be sceptical, or even scornful, of anything alleged on behalf of the humanities which appeared to them sentimental or conventional,—and were little disposed to conserve any element in education to which they could not assign a definite rational value. As a typical expression of those tendencies, one might mention the volume of 'Essays on a Liberal Education,' published in 1867.

In the sixties, then, considering the strength of the attack both from without and from within, the position of humane studies was certainly more seriously imperilled than it had ever been before. Not, indeed, that even then there was any danger of their being discarded at once. But there was a danger of another kind. Some influential men were saying, 'Keep Latin if you like, but drop Greek, or reserve it for a few boys ; and take care that the classics do not, in any case, trench upon the time which should, in all schools, be given to natural science and to modern studies.' The danger was lest the powerful alliance between insurgent men of science and disaffected humanists, aided by the legions of Philistia, should force on a movement for imposing such restrictions as these in a spirit altogether favourable to the new studies, but un-friendly to the old ;—with the result that classical studies might be so narrowed, so hampered, so maimed, as to lose nearly all their distinctive educational virtue ; and, after languishing for a time, might gradually die out of the schools.

That danger was sensibly increased by a further circumstance. It was the first time in England that classical education had been seriously put upon its defence ; and some of its less discreet defenders made some claims on its behalf which were ill-founded or exaggerated. Thus one eminent scholar said, ' If the old classical literature were swept away, the moderns would in many cases become unintelligible, and in all cases lose most of their characteristic charms.' Others averred that no one could write English well who did not know Latin. One distinguished head-master even said, ' It is scarcely possible to speak the English language with accuracy or precision, without a knowledge of Latin or Greek.' Now claims of this kind, all containing some elements of truth, but needing to be carefully limited and defined, struck people in general as preposterous, when stated with crude exaggeration ; and did all the more mischief, because, in the sixties, an apprehension of the true claims of humanism was much less widely diffused, among educated people outside of the academic world, than it is to-day. And when such people, who had no personal knowledge of humanistic study, heard claims made for it which seemed repugnant to experience and common-sense, they not unnaturally suspected that the whole case for the humanities was unsound.

But in the last thirty years the position of the humane letters, relatively to other studies, has been altered in several important respects. The study of the natural sciences is now firmly established in schools and universities ; it can no longer be said that a haughty and exclusive humanism keeps them out of the educational field : indeed, there are not a few seats of learning where they hold a clear predominance. Modern languages and literatures have also their recognised place in the higher education ; if they do not yet attract as many disciples as they deserve, the reason is not that they are neglected or discouraged by educational authorities, but rather that they are new studies, with methods and aims which are still in some measure tentative, and competing with highly equipped rivals of older standing. This establishment of the modern studies is, so far as I have seen, viewed by humanists generally with cordial satisfaction. The spirit of humanism, indeed, wherever it is not a narrow pedantry, is one which welcomes every accession to the domain of sound knowledge. Meanwhile, the claims of humanism itself, sifted by a period of controversy, and illustrated by the larger views of liberal education which now prevail, are usually stated with more discrimination than formerly, and are more willingly and more widely acknowledged.

Now, what are the true and permanent claims of humanistic studies ? They are of two kinds, the intrinsic, and the historical. The intrinsic merits of the classical literatures depend, in the first place, on

Present position of humanism.

Its permanent claims.

their purely literary qualities in respect to form and
style.   The creative literature of Greece, from
Homer to Demosthenes, had a course of spontaneous
and natural growth, throughout which it was in
constant touch with life ; and it has left a series of
typical standards in prose and poetry.   The excellence of these models is not a scholastic figment or
a medieval superstition ; it is a fact which has been
recognised, through all the changes of the centuries,
by the common feeling and the general consent of
civilised mankind.   The Roman literature, though
partly imitative, is not only original in some of its
types, but original throughout as a manifestation
of the Latin genius in the speech which that genius
moulded ; and abounds in works of poetry and
prose which must always rank as masterpieces.   An
unguarded champion of the classics once said of
them that 'they utterly condemn all false ornament,
all tinsel, all ungraceful and unshapely work.'   That
statement, though quite true in a general sense, is
not true without exception ; the classics are not
perfect, any more than other human productions ;
they have their occasional faults or blemishes in
style and taste.   But it would argue a strange de-
ficiency in the sense of proportion, a singular want
of balance in literary judgment, to affirm that such
faults or blemishes detract in any appreciable degree
from the intellectual stimulus and the æsthetic pleasure which their great and characteristic qualities
afford, or from the admiration due to the artistic
harmony of their best work, when viewed as a

whole. The utility of the classical languages as subjects of study and as instruments of training depends partly on these qualities of the literatures, but also on the importance of these languages themselves for grammar and comparative philology. They afford, moreover, a discipline in nicety of judgment which is all the better because the questions of idiom and usage which they raise cannot be solved by living authority.

The intrinsic value of the classical literatures depends, further, on their contents. The claim made for them on this score at the present day is much more limited than that which was made by the humanists of the Renaissance ; but, within those limits, it is as valid as ever. The observations and discoveries of the Greeks and Romans in particular sciences, such as Mathematics or Medicine, have been incorporated or transmuted in modern work, and no longer form a practical reason for studying the literatures, though still investing them with a special interest for some students who would not otherwise be drawn to them. But an universal and abiding interest belongs to another and far larger element in their contents. That element is the store of experience and observation accumulated by keen watchers of human nature and conduct through all the centuries from Homer to Justinian. And the utterance of this varied wisdom of life is precisely one of the regions in which the distinctive excellences of classical expression shine most. This is a kind of literary wealth which, as John Stuart

Mill said of it, 'does not well admit of being transferred bodily' into modern books, and 'has been
very imperfectly transferred even piecemeal.'

The historical value of the classical literatures is
that which arises from their relation to the modern.
No one, of course, would now maintain that a
knowledge of Greek or Latin is necessary to success
in writing English; such a statement could be dis-
proved by a cloud of witnesses,—among others, by
Shakespeare, De Foe, Bunyan, Byron, Carlyle,
Cobbett, Charles Lamb. But it is certain that no
one can comprehend the history and development
of English literature, or of any literature of modern
Europe, without a knowledge of the ultimate sources
in ancient Greece and Italy. Without such a knowledge, the process by which the forms of modern
literature have been evolved would be unintelligible.
It has been urged, indeed, that for a student of a
modern literature the important thing is to know the
immediate antecedents of that literature, rather than
the more remote; and that, if the student of English
literature, for instance, studies Early English, it is
needless to trouble him with Greek or Latin. It
may be replied, however, that, in the study of modern
literary history, the light afforded by the nearer past
differs in kind from that which is given by the more
distant past. The nearer past will explain details;
as a study of Chaucer will give the key to some later
forms or usages of the language. But it is necessary
to go further back,—in the case of any European
literature, it is necessary to go back to ancient Greece

and Italy, if you desire to find the points from which
the main currents of literary tradition started, and
from which the chief types in literature have been
derived. An ordinary reader does not require to
know the classics in order to appreciate and enjoy
modern literature, though such knowledge will en-
hance his appreciation and enjoyment at many points.
But, for any one who aspires to be a scholarly critic
of modern literature, the knowledge is indispensable.

Finally, it should not be forgotten that classical
literature affords the best, if not a necessary, pre-
paration for the study of classical art; and that
Greek art remains, in its own province, the most
perfect expression of the artistic spirit.

Such, in outline, are the principal claims that
can be made for the humanities. These merits
surely entitle them to keep their place in the higher
literary education. I do not think that there is any
exaggeration in what Mr Froude said thirteen years
ago, that, if we ever lose those studies, 'our national
taste, and the tone of our national intellect, will
suffer a serious decline.' Classical studies help to
preserve sound standards of literature. It is not
difficult to lose such standards, even for a nation
with the highest material civilisation, with abounding
mental activity, and with a great literature of its own.
It is peculiarly easy to do so in days when the
lighter and more ephemeral kinds of writing form
for many people the staple of daily reading. The
fashions of the hour may start a movement, not in
the best direction, which may go on until the path is

Humanism as a safe-guard of literary standards.

difficult to retrace. The humanities, if they cannot
prevent such a movement, can do something to
temper and counteract it; because they appeal to
permanent things, to the instinct for beauty in
human nature, and to the emotions; and in any
one who is at all susceptible to their influence
they develope a literary conscience. Nor is this
all. Their power in the higher education will affect
the quality of the literary teaching lower down.
Every one can see how vitally important it is for us,
in this country and at this moment, to maintain, in
our general education, a proper balance of subjects,
and to secure that, while scientific and technical
studies have full scope, a due efficacy shall be given
also to the studies of literature and history.

We have no Academy of Letters in England,
and, for my part, I am with those who hope that we
never shall have one. But no doubt we must desire
to have what Mr Matthew Arnold called 'a public
force of correct literary opinion, possessing within
certain limits a clear sense of what is right and
wrong, sound and unsound.' In concluding this
lecture, I would venture to say that such a force of
correct literary opinion is just what an intelligent
humanism should contribute to supply; not, as an
Academy does, in a public or corporate form, but
through the influence and example of individuals.
Humanism can do that, if it is loyal to its best self;
if it avoids a needless excess of technicality in the
treatment of literature; if it cultivates sanity of
judgment, and is careful that the exercise of

ingenuity shall be controlled by the literary sense. Discoveries of a signal kind, such as mark the progress of the new sciences, can seldom now be expected in the province of humanism. In humanism the genuine originality must now consist, for the most part, in applying, by patient work, a more accurate knowledge and a more delicate perception at a number of particular points, in the hope of enabling each successive generation of students to apprehend classical antiquity in a more fruitful manner, with a greater distinctness and with a nearer approach to truth.

It has been a great privilege for me to address such an audience on this subject. I am well aware how little I have had to say that can be new to many of my hearers; but it may be good sometimes, in the case of studies which are so important for the intellectual well-being of the nation, to pause and think what they mean and where they stand; to look back and to look forward. The endeavour to do so, however defective the result may be, is at least one which cannot be foreign to the traditions or the genius of the place in which I have had the honour to speak.

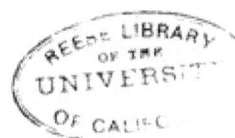

CAMBRIDGE: PRINTED BY J. & C. F. CLAY, AT THE UNIVERSITY PRESS.